# BEGINNING CELLIST'S SONGBOOK

## MB21880

## BY JOE MARONI

*Visit us on the Web at www.melbay.com or www.billsmusicshelf.com*

# Contents

**Title**                                                                 **Page**

Introduction                                                                    3
The Wearing of the Green                                                         4
Greensleeves                                                                     5
Flowers of Edinburgh                                                             6
Londonderry Air                                                                  7
Nearer My God, to Thee                                                          8
Chester                                                                         9
Come Back to Sorrento                                                           10
Ode to Joy                                                                      11
The Wayfaring Stranger                                                          12
Aura Lee                                                                        13
Stack of Barley                                                                 14
We Gather Together                                                              15
Whispering Hope                                                                 16
Where the River Shannon Flows                                                   17
All Through the Night                                                           18
Yankee Doodle                                                                   19
Big Rock Candy Mountain                                                         20
The Cowboy's Lament (Streets of Laredo)                                         21
Alouette                                                                        22
When the Work's All Done in the Fall                                            23
Long, Long Ago                                                                  24
Minuet                                                                          25
Home on the Range                                                               26
Faith of Our Fathers                                                           27

# Introduction

The purpose of this cellist songbook is to provide the beginning cellist with a repertoire of 24 of the most familiar and beloved tunes ever written. There are several great folk songs of America and other lands. They continue to bring pleasure and knowledge as a link to the past.

All the songs are written specifically for cello utilizing dynamics, expression markings, and articulations. Key signatures for the songs are in a comfortable range suitable for the beginning cellist. Guitar chord symbols appear above each melody, however, the chords may be played by banjo, ukulele, autoharp, and chord organ.

Included are: Irish Songs, Folk Songs, American Hymns, Spirituals, and Classics.

This song book is an ideal supplement to *"Cello Method"* (MB96459) published by Mel Bay Publications, Inc.

All the songs are appropriate for performance at concerts, recitals, and contests.

# The Wearing of the Green

# Greensleeves

Old English Folk Song

# Flowers of Edinburgh

## Hornpipe

Irish Air

# Londonderry Air

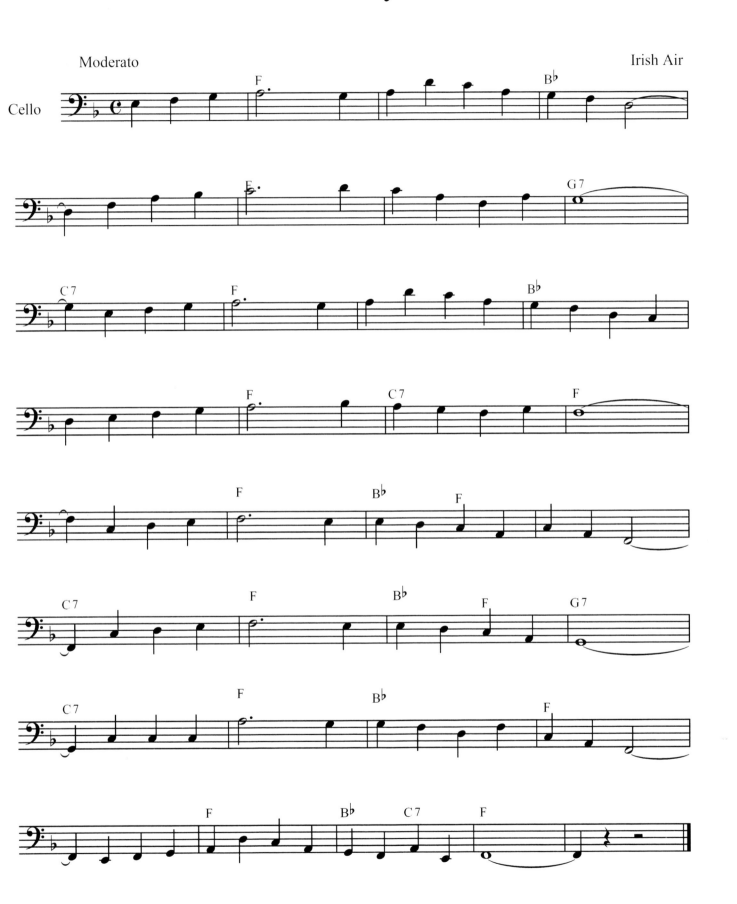

# Nearer My God ,To Thee

# Chester

# Come Back to Sorrento

# Ode to Joy

From the Ninth Symphony

Ludwig Van Beethoven

# The Wayfaring Stranger

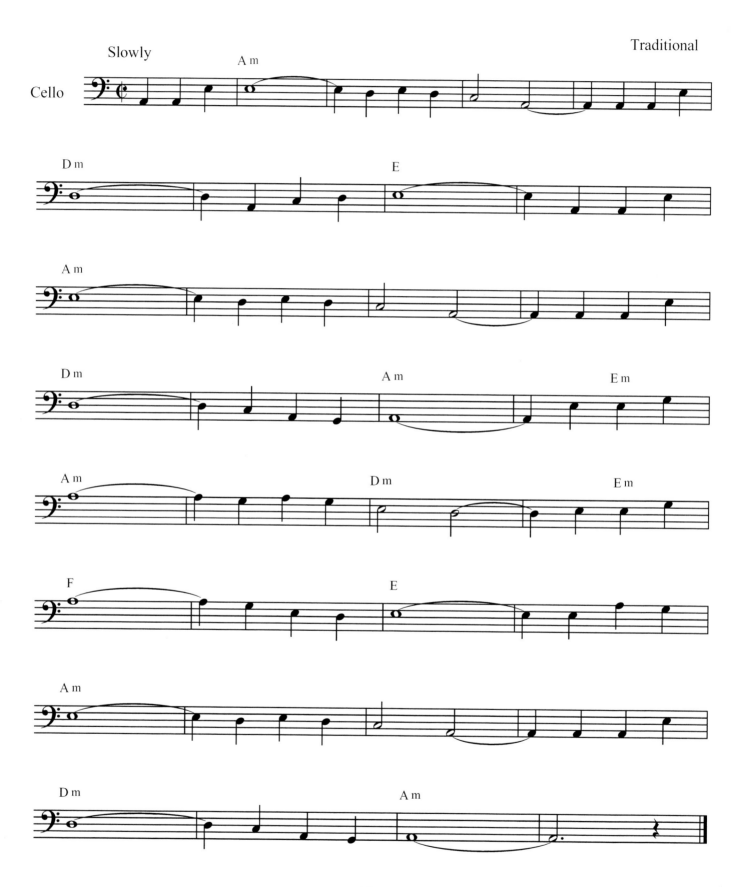

# Aura Lee

# Stack of Barley

# We Gather Together

# Whispering Hope

Hymn

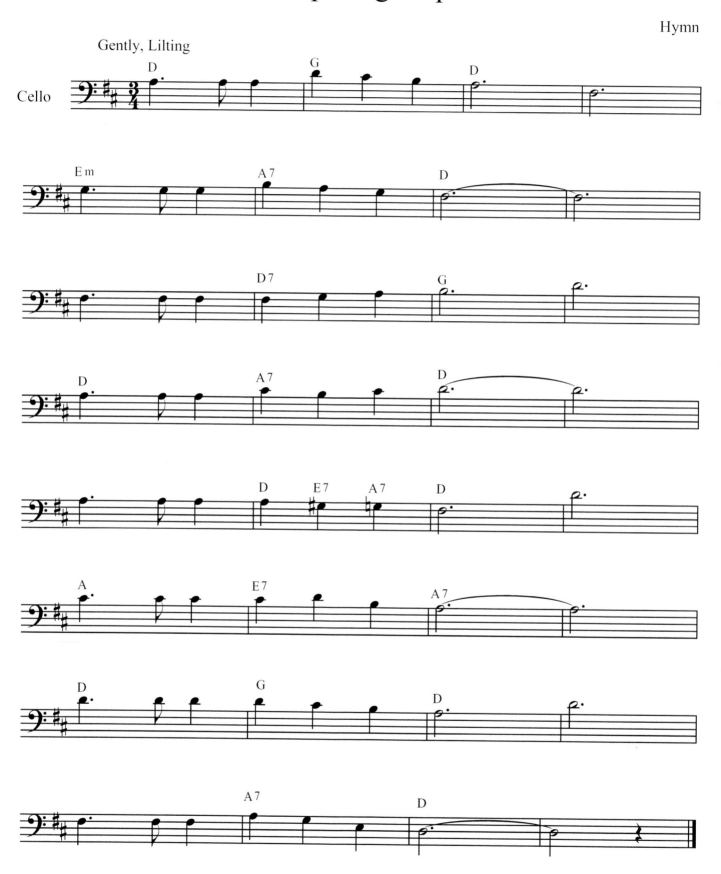

16

# Where The River Shannon Flows

# All Through the Night

Welsh Folk Song

18

# Yankee Dooodle

# Big Rock Candy Mountain

# The Cowboy's Lament

## The Streets of Laredo

Old American Western Song

# Alouette

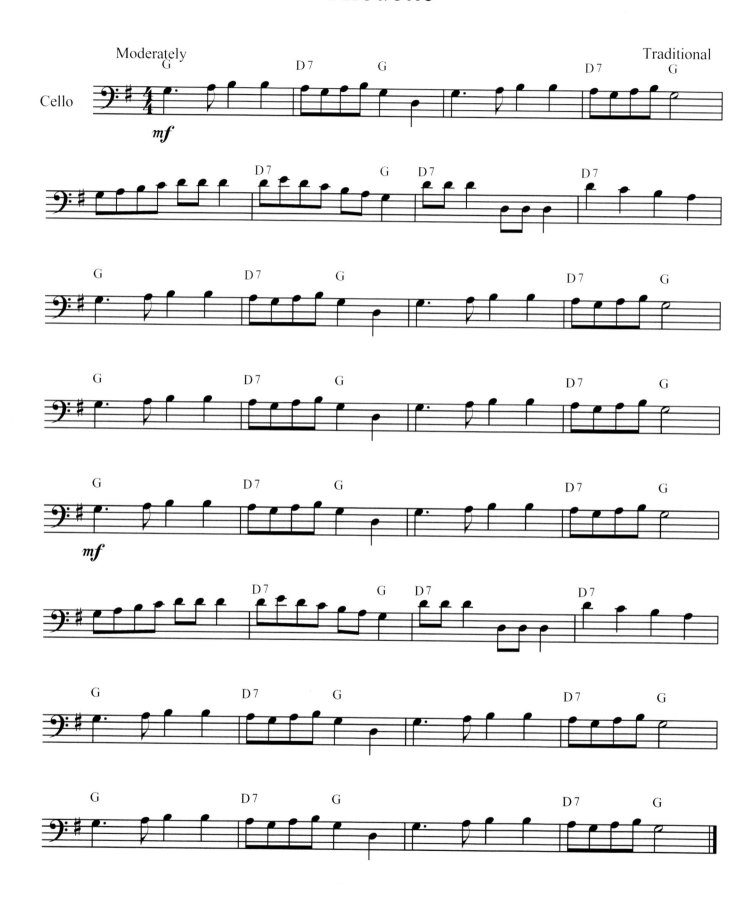

# When the Work's All Done This Fall

# Long, Long Ago

Moderately

Old America Folk Song

# Minuet

Johann Sebastian Bach

# Home on the Range

# Faith of Our Fathers

*Joe Maroni*

# Other Cello Books by Joe Maroni

## MB21945 101 Easy Songs for Cello